CRAZY HARD PATTERNS

BY

TABZ JONES

FIRST EDITION 2016

TABZ JONES
PO BOX 2137
ALMA, AR. 72921
WWW.GOTHICTOGGS.NET

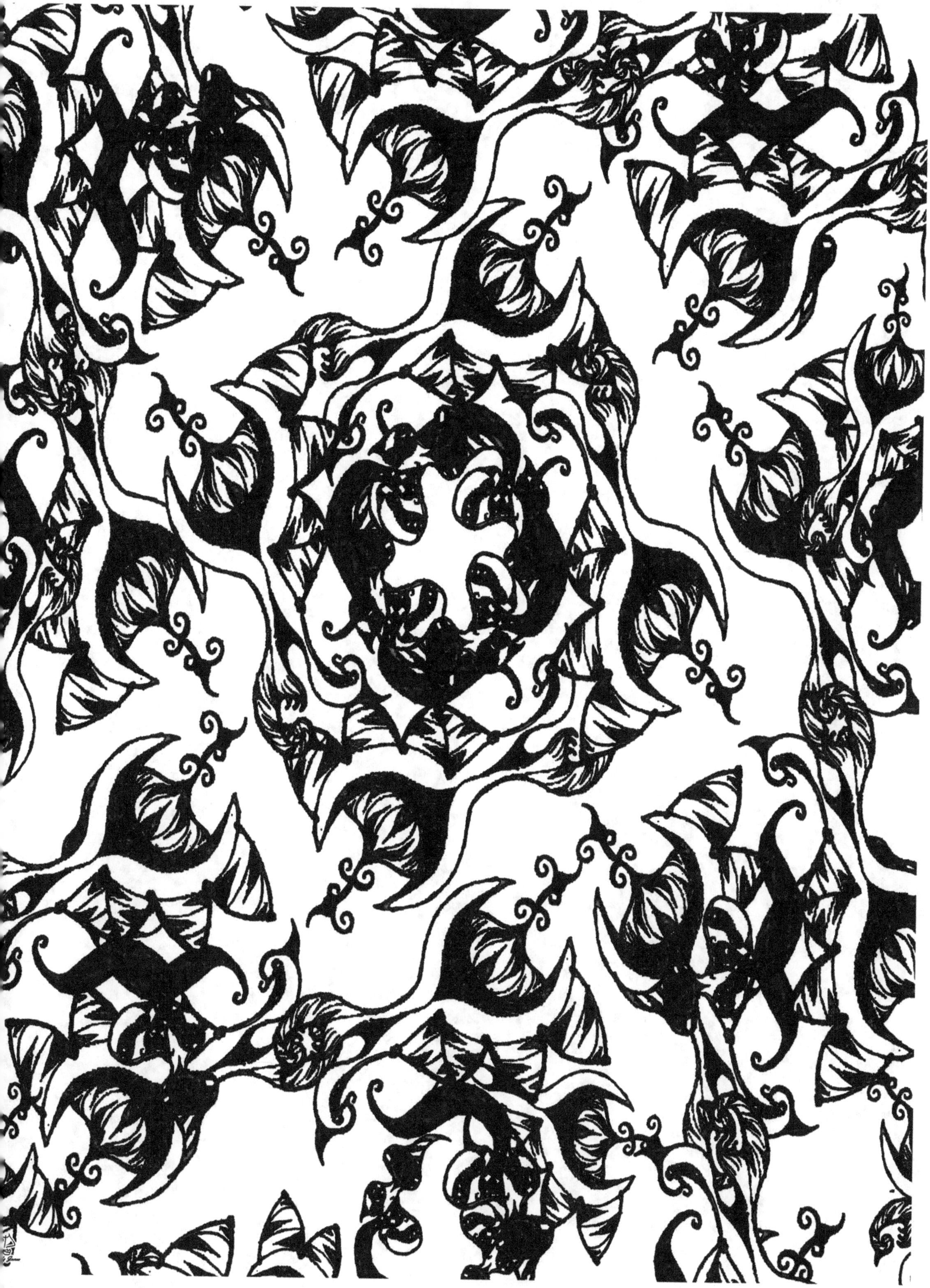

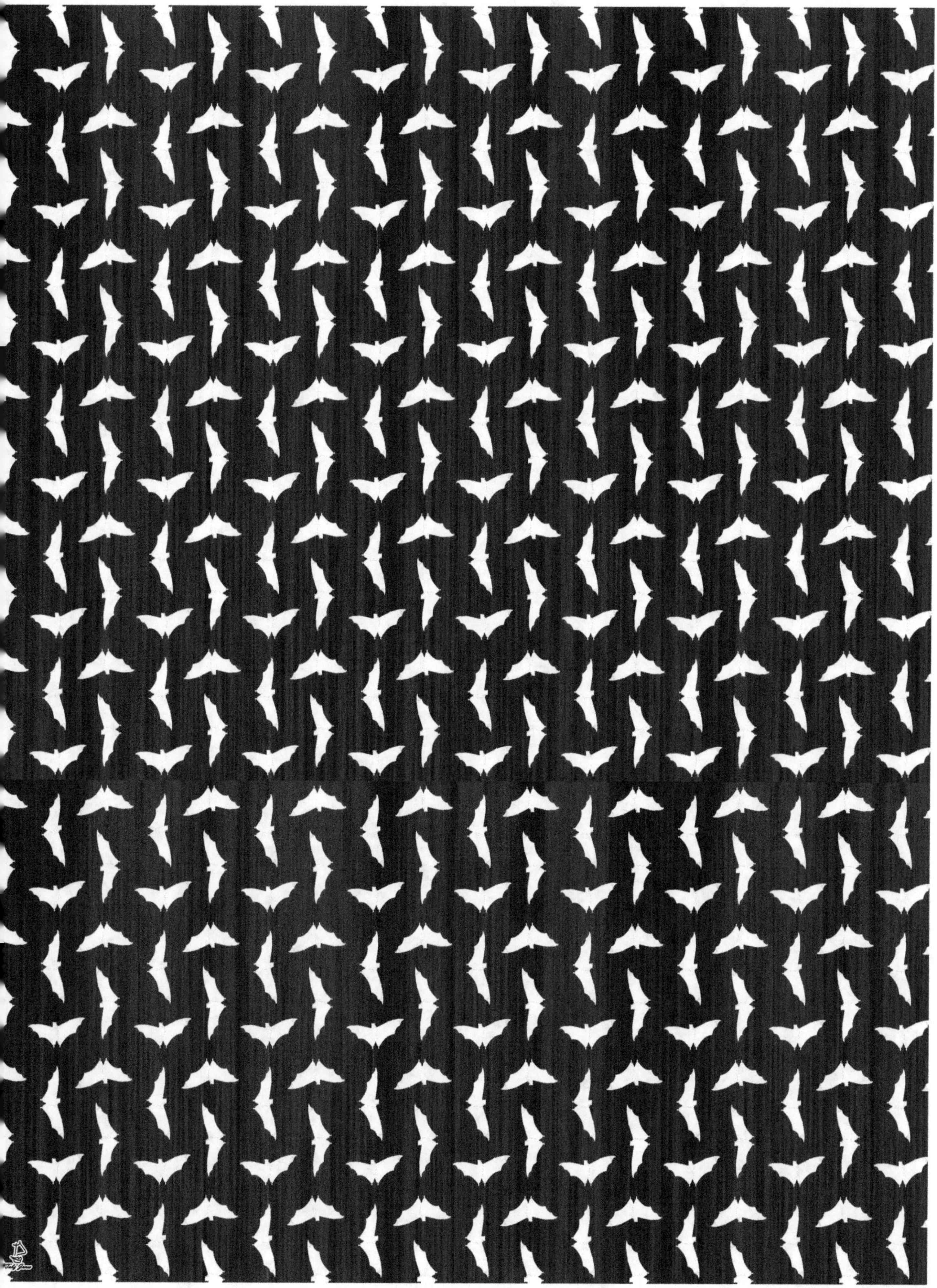

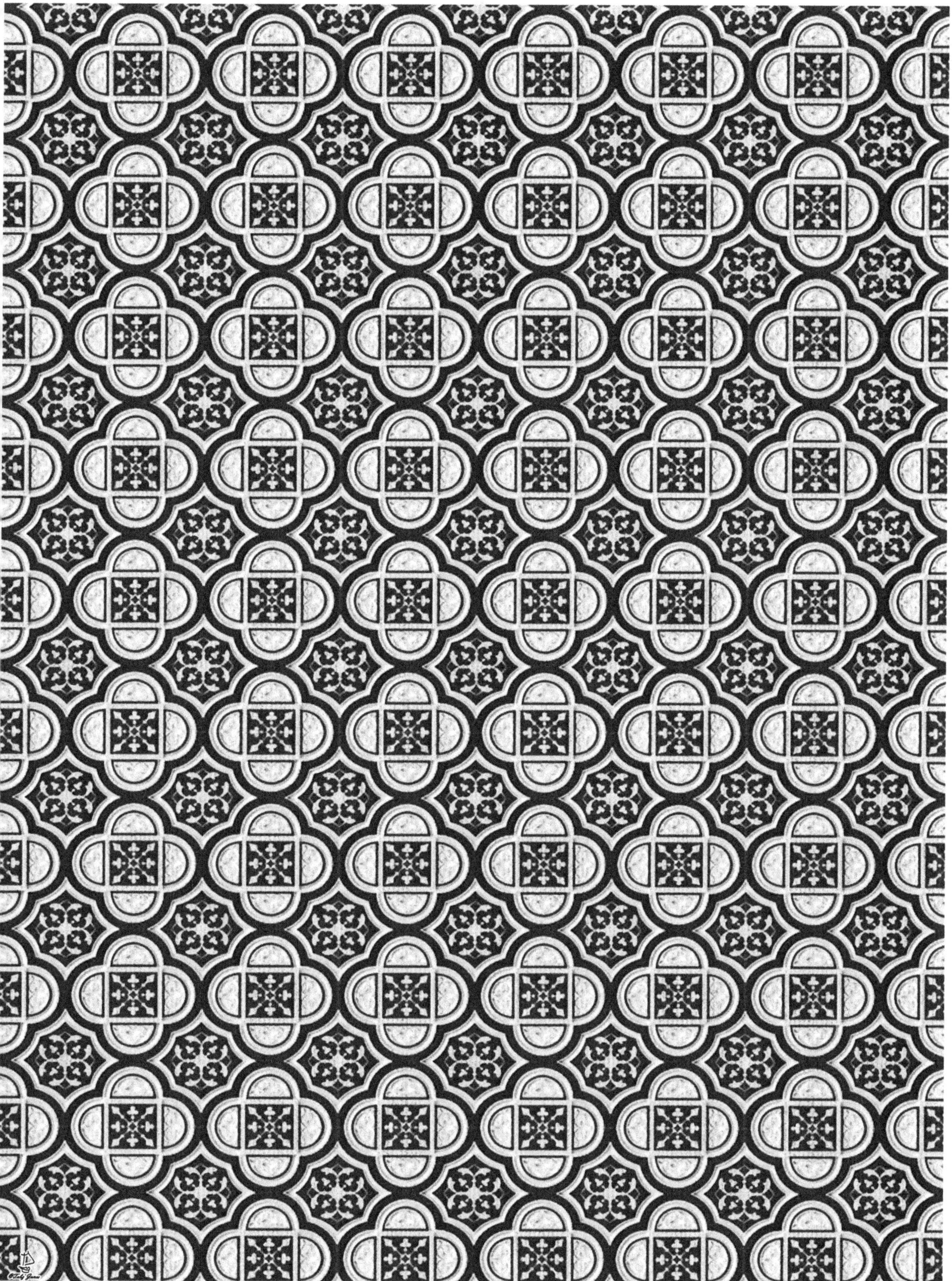

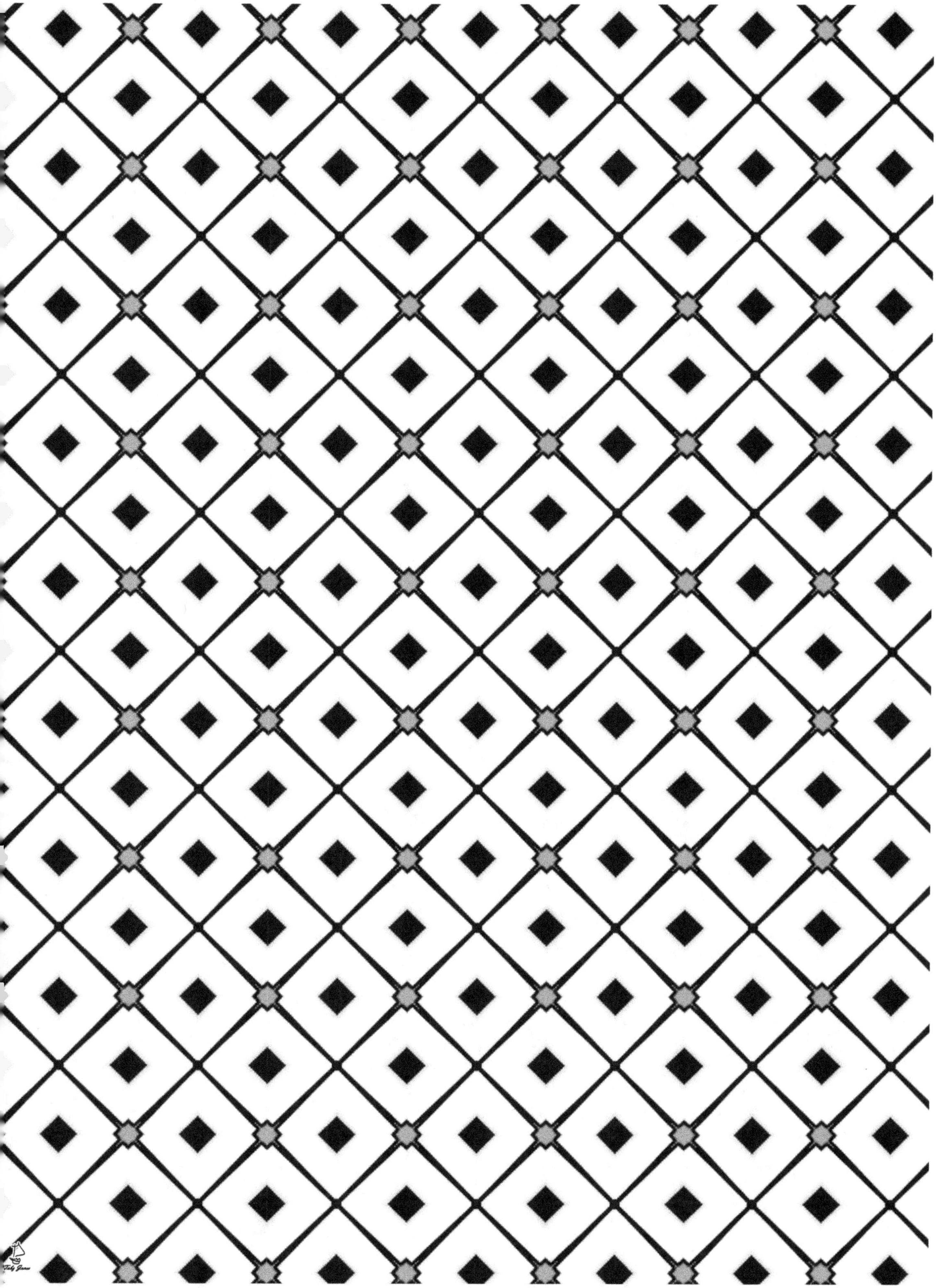

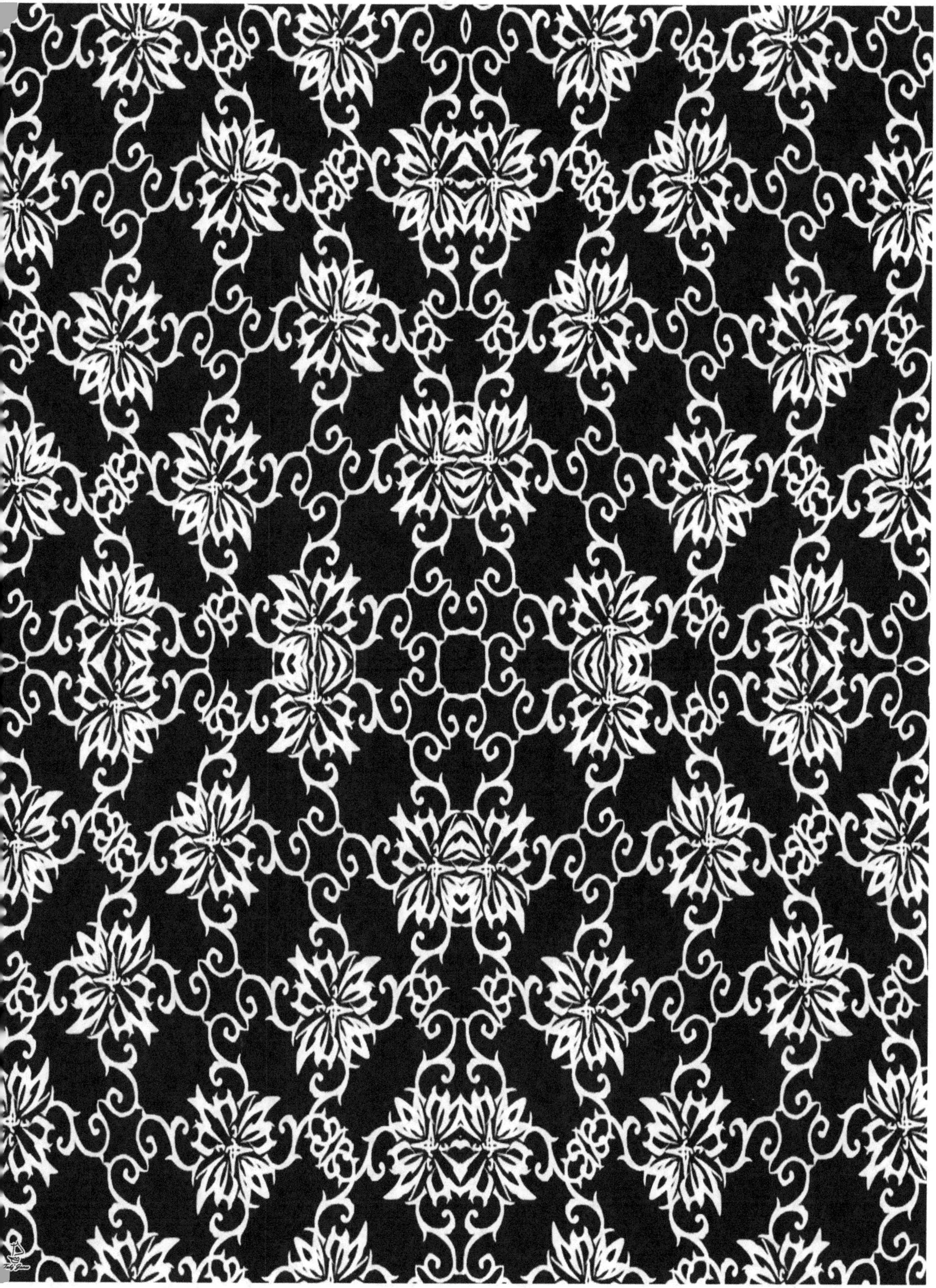

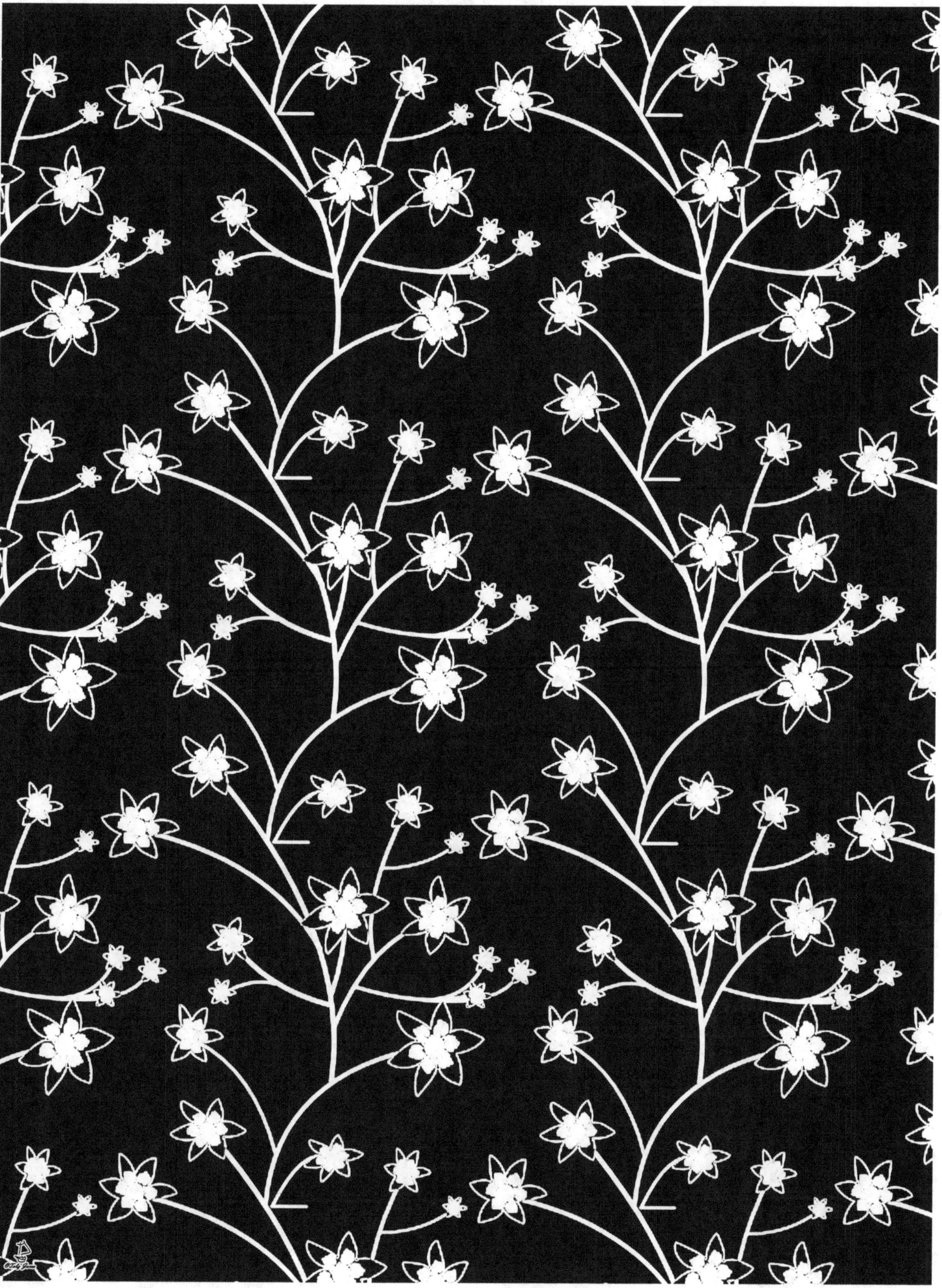

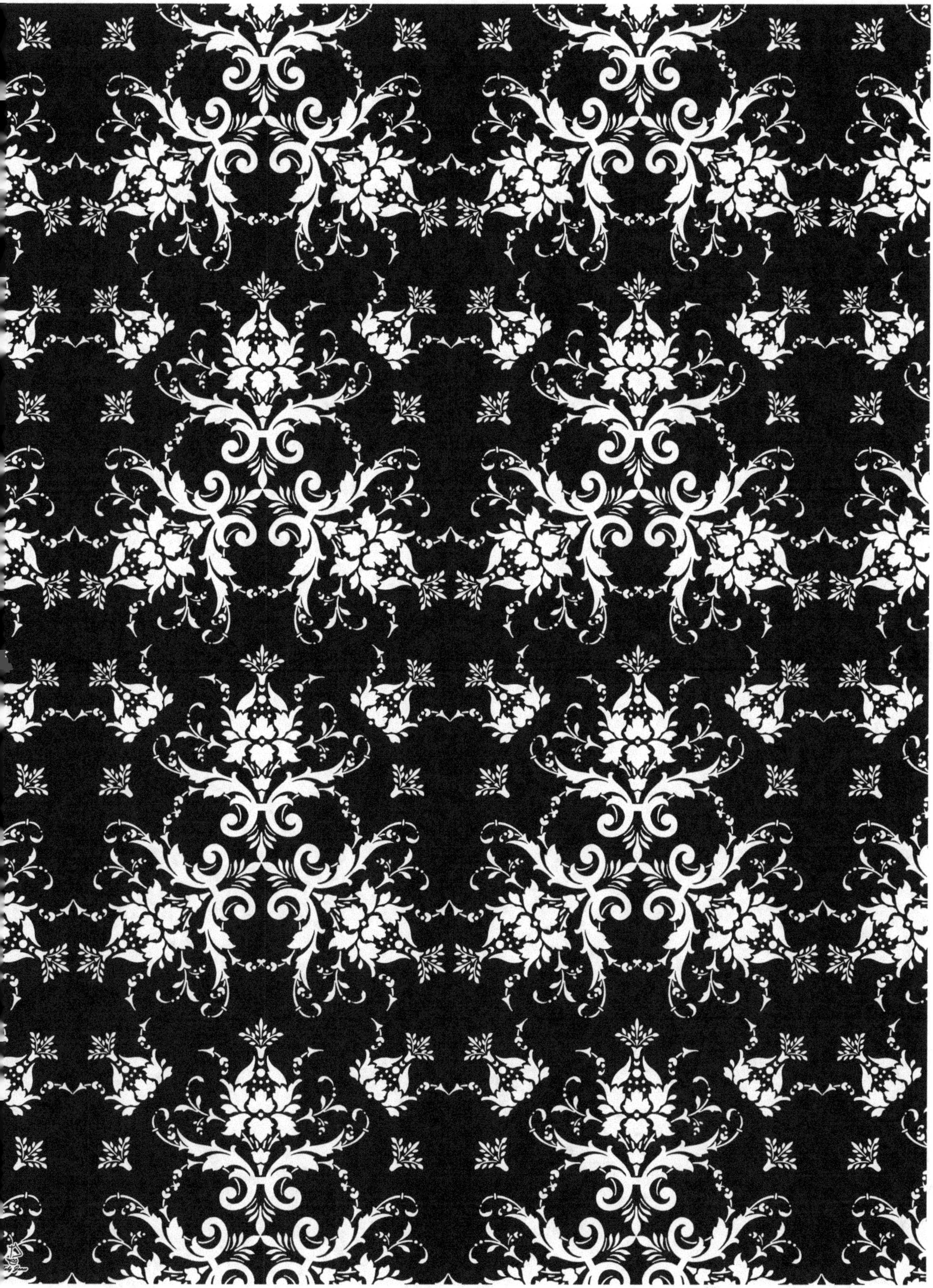

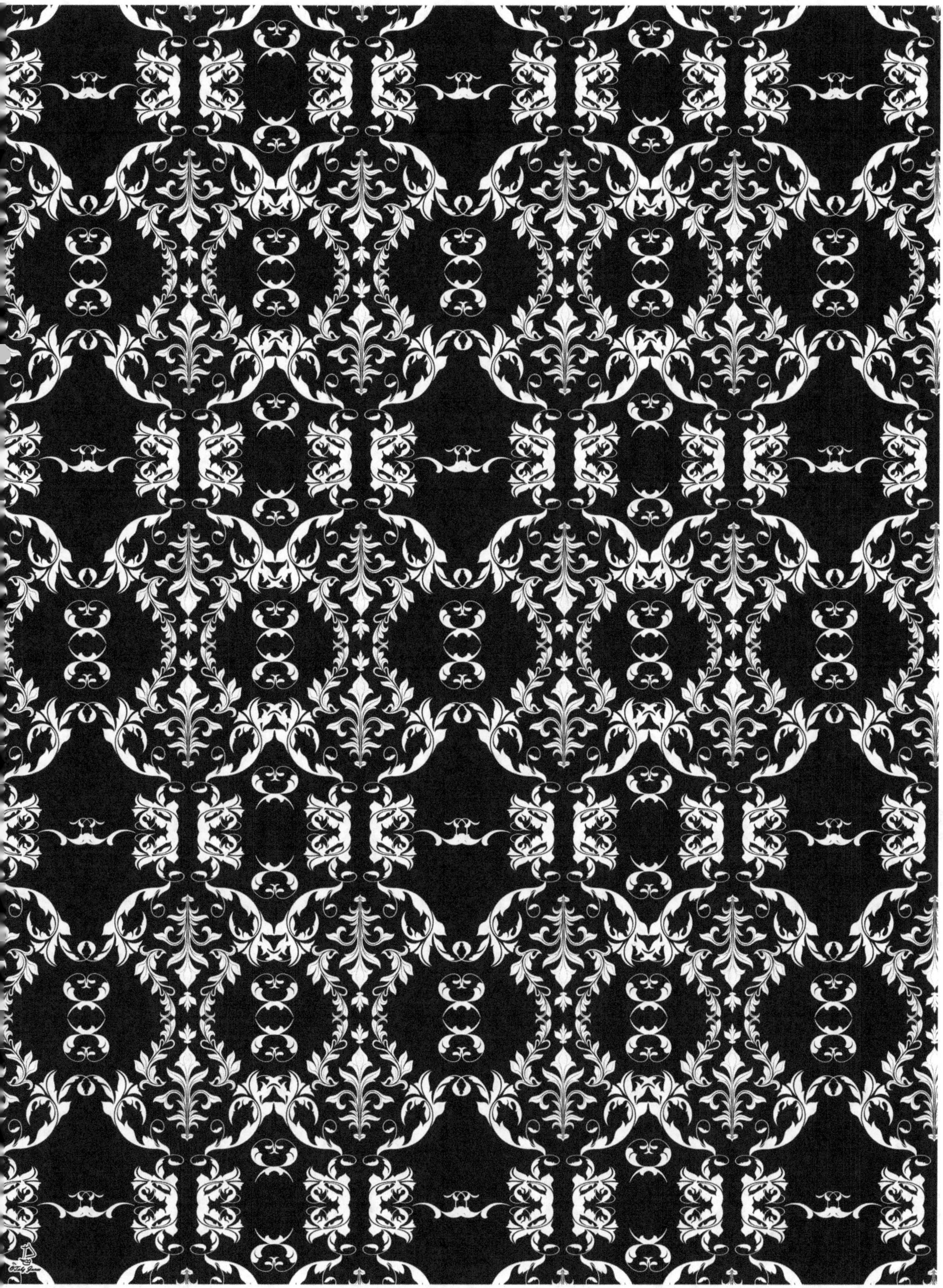

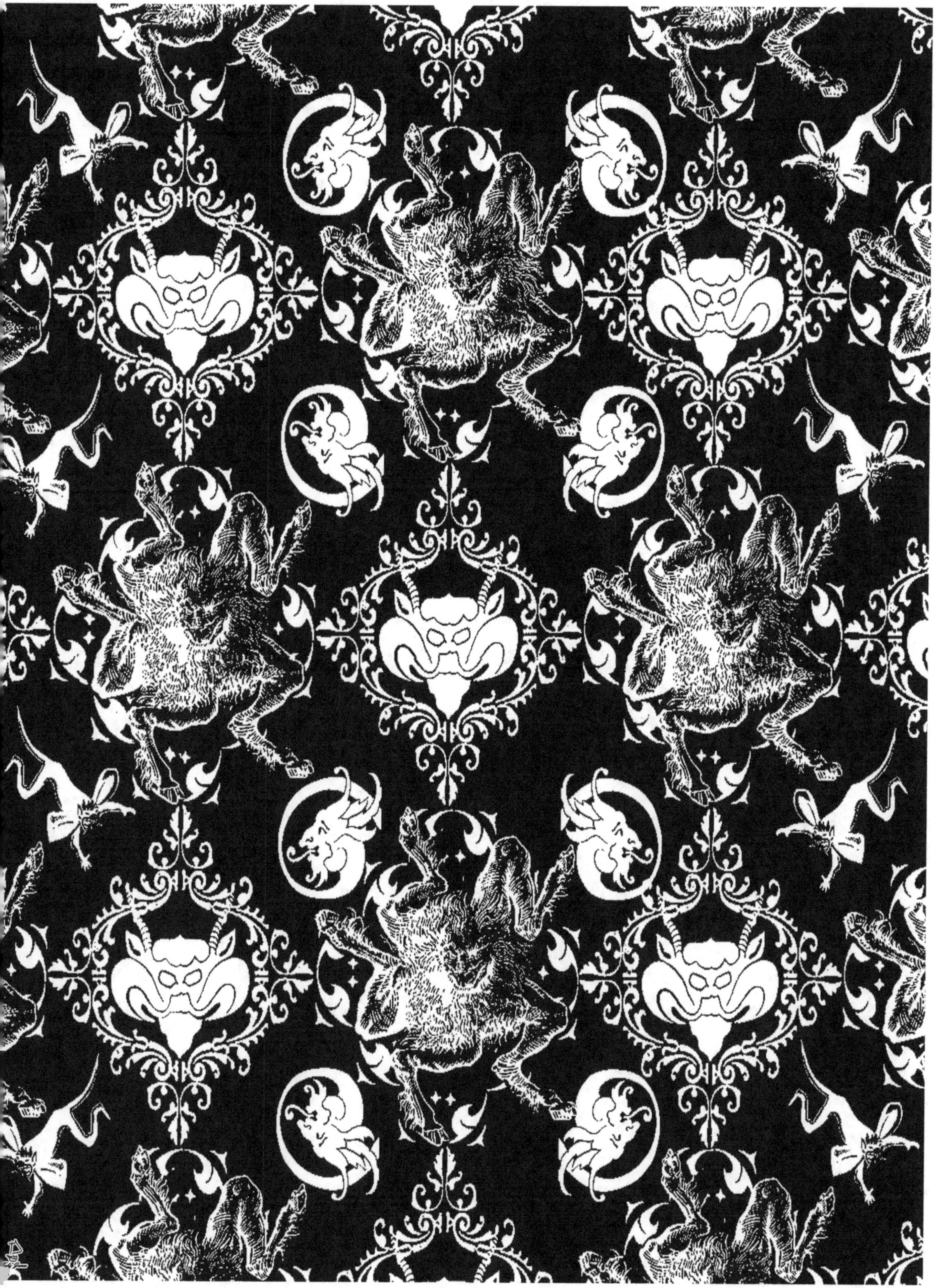

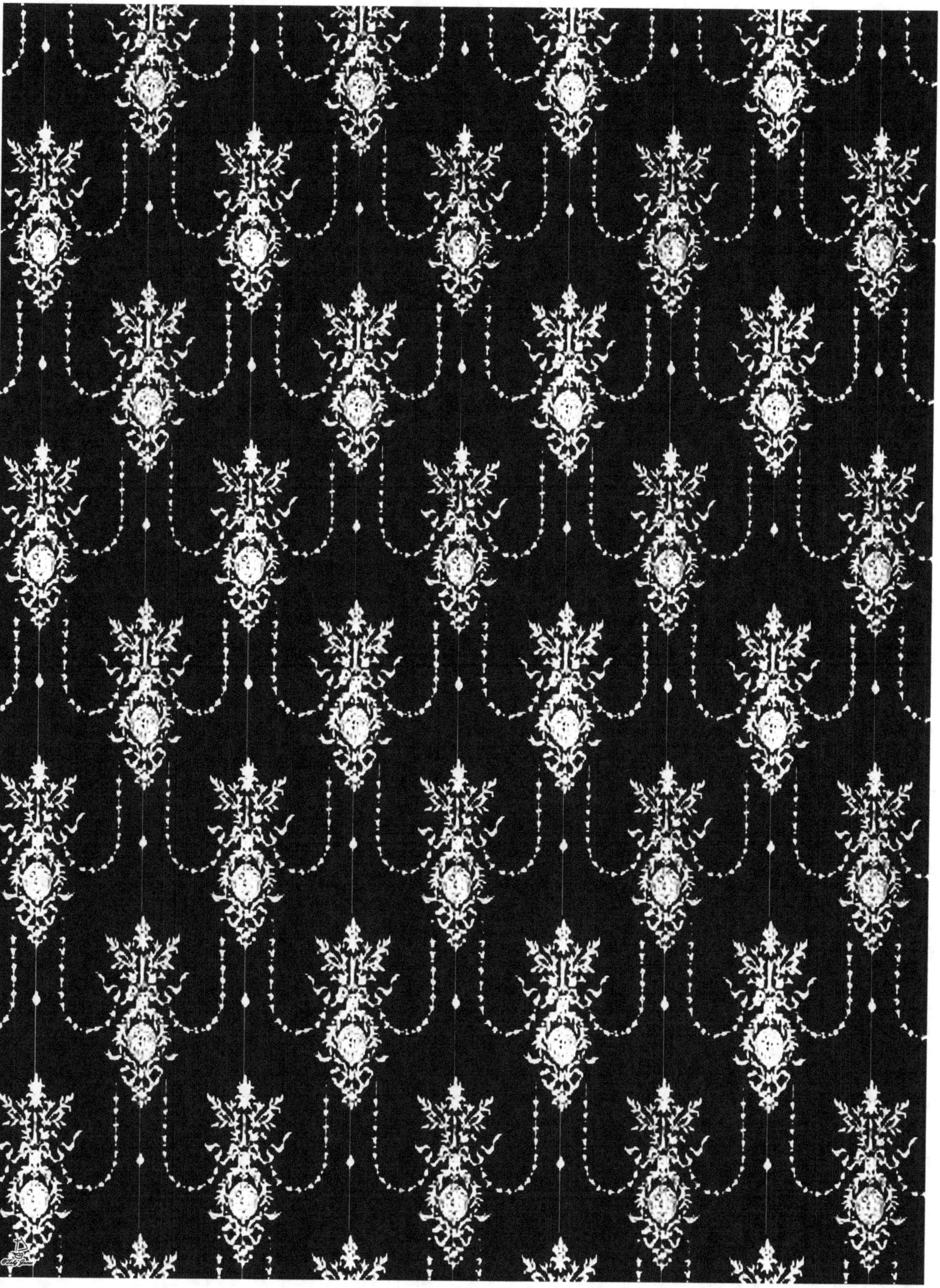

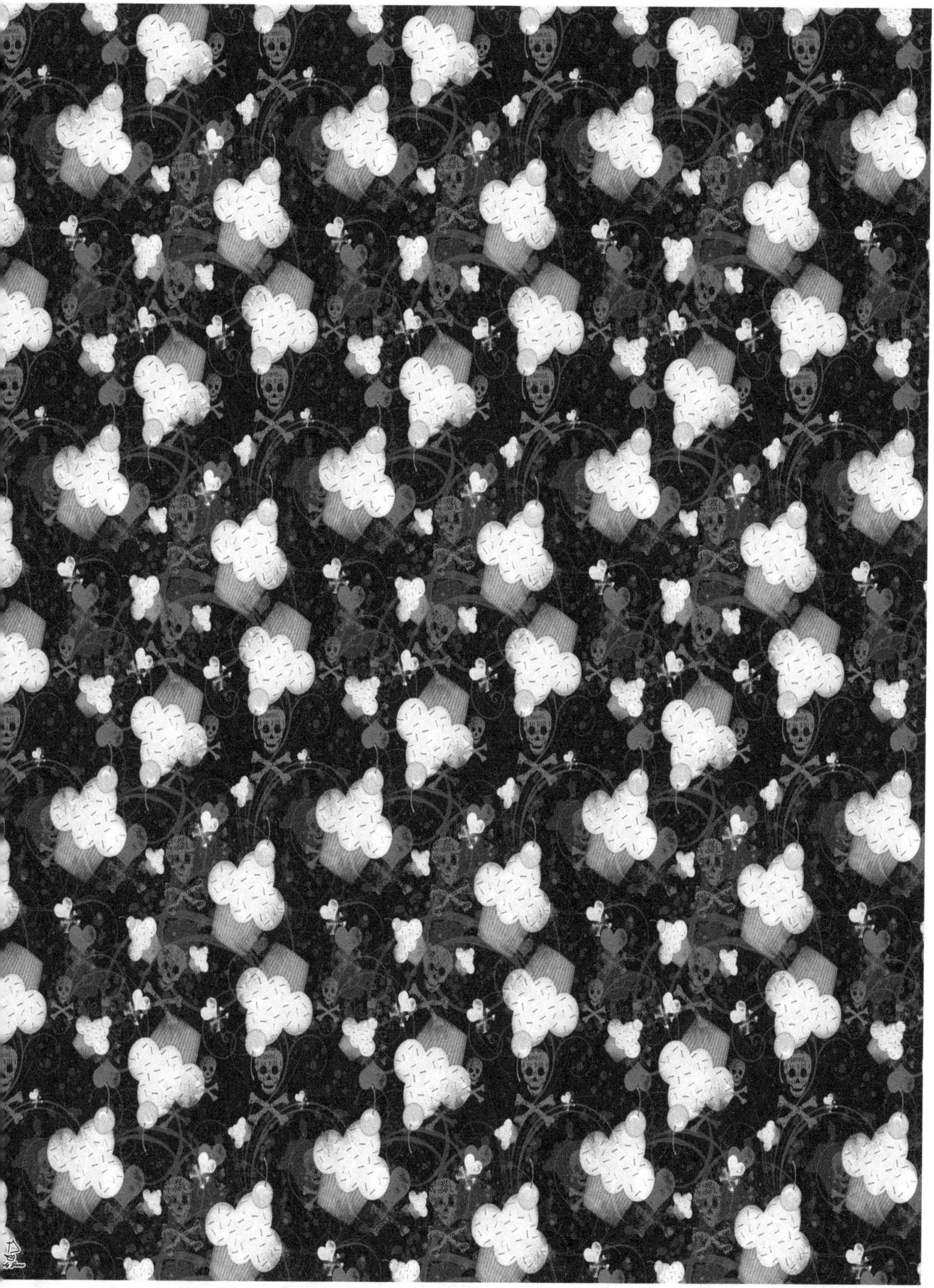

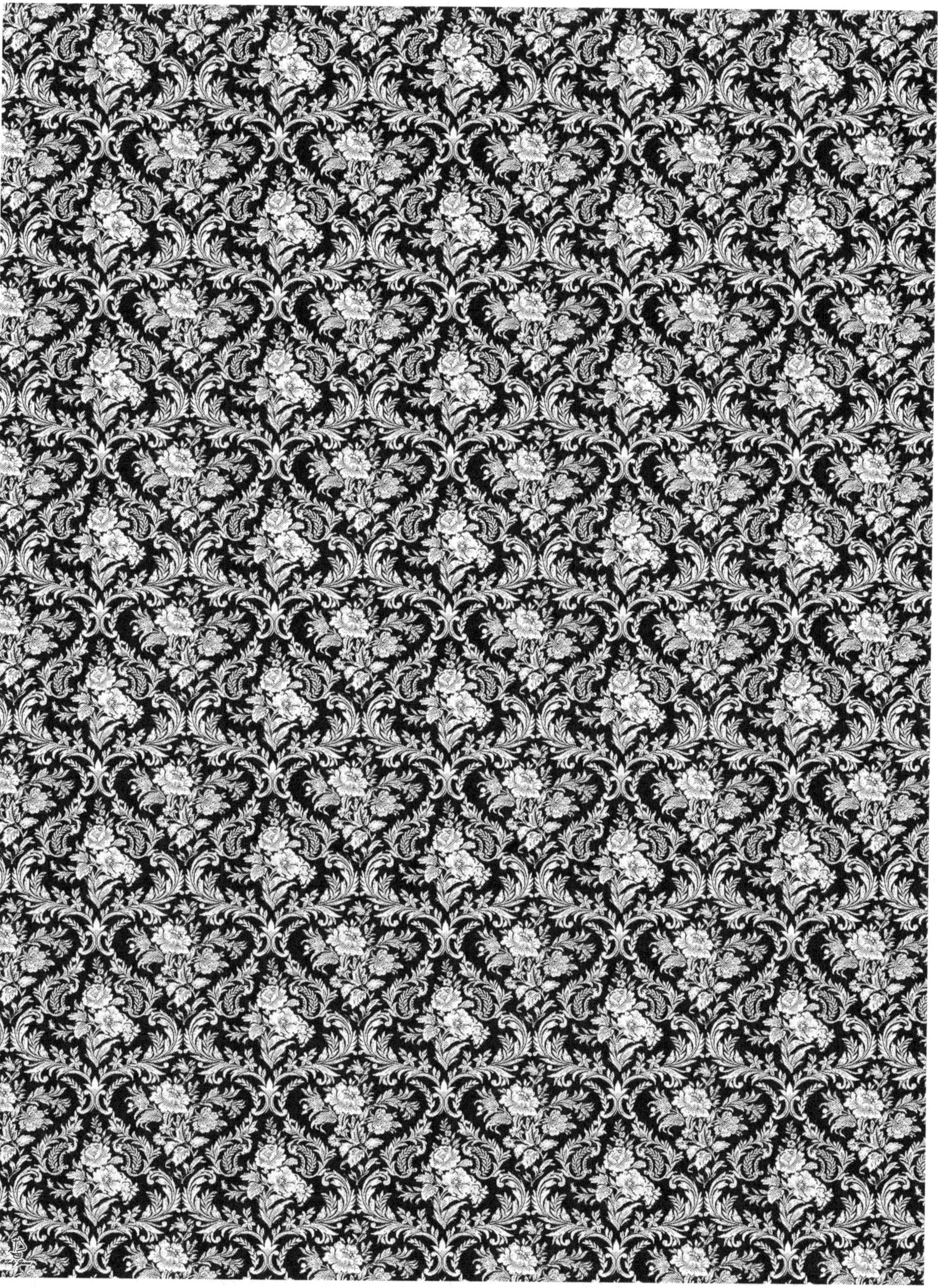

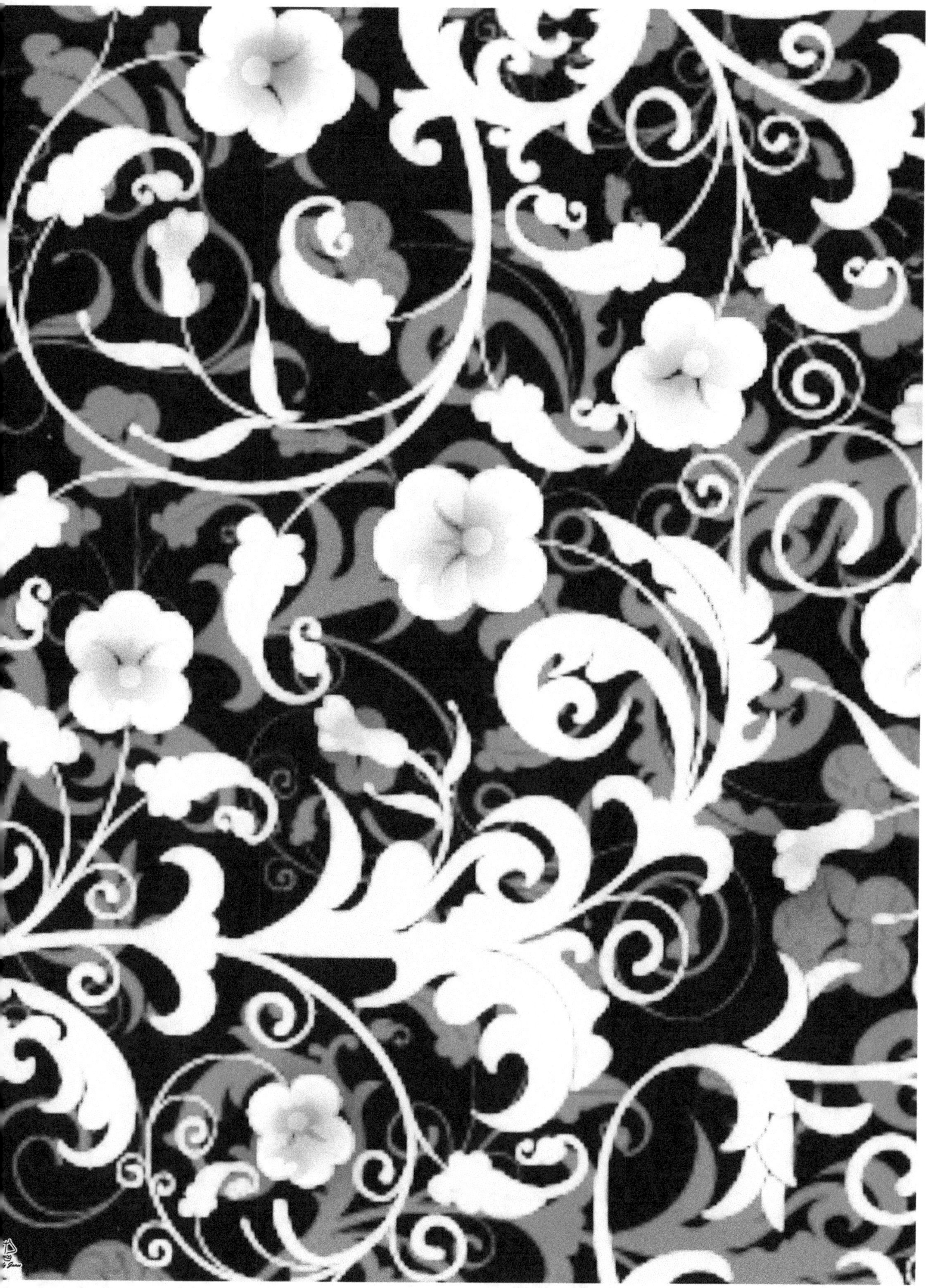

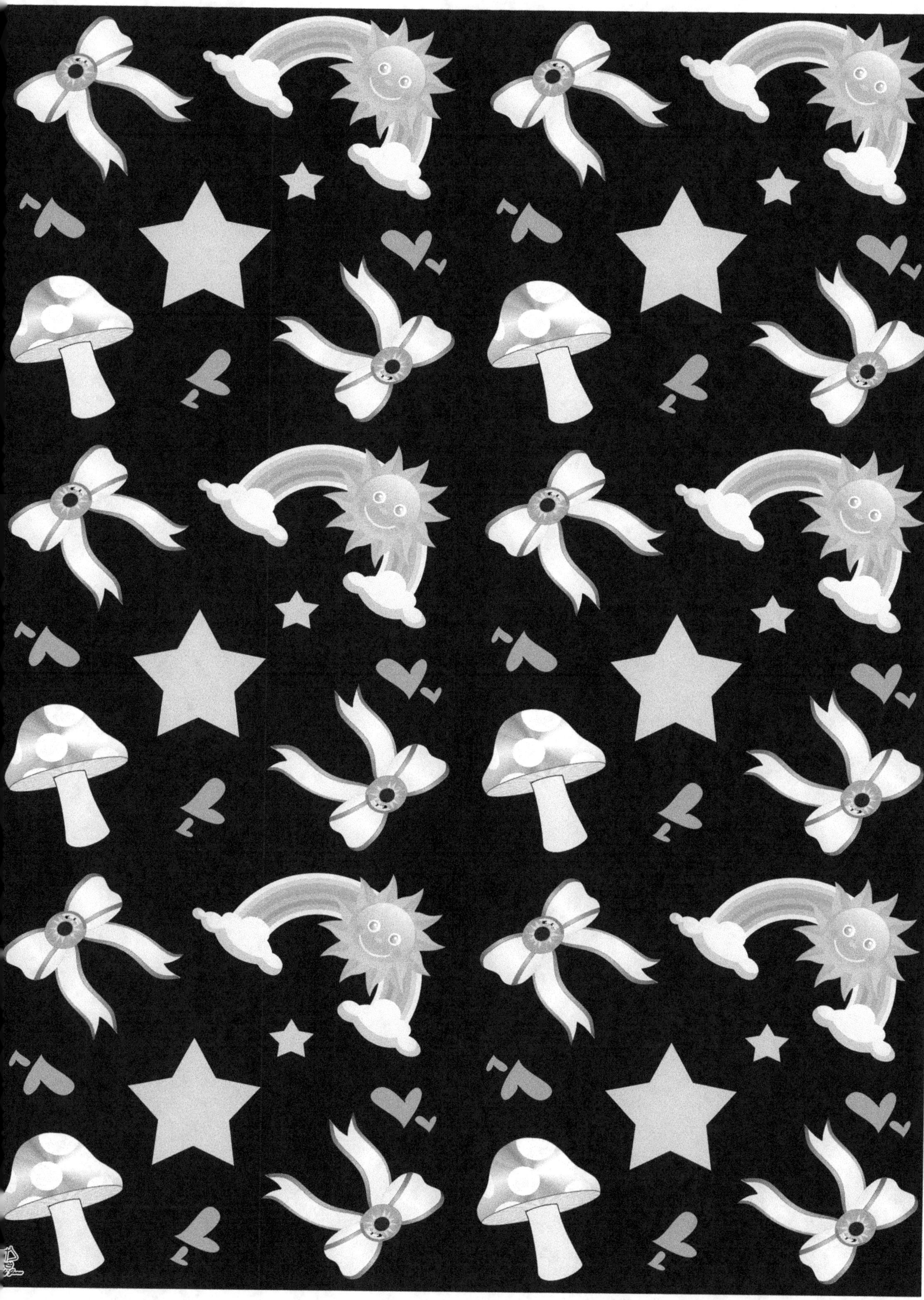

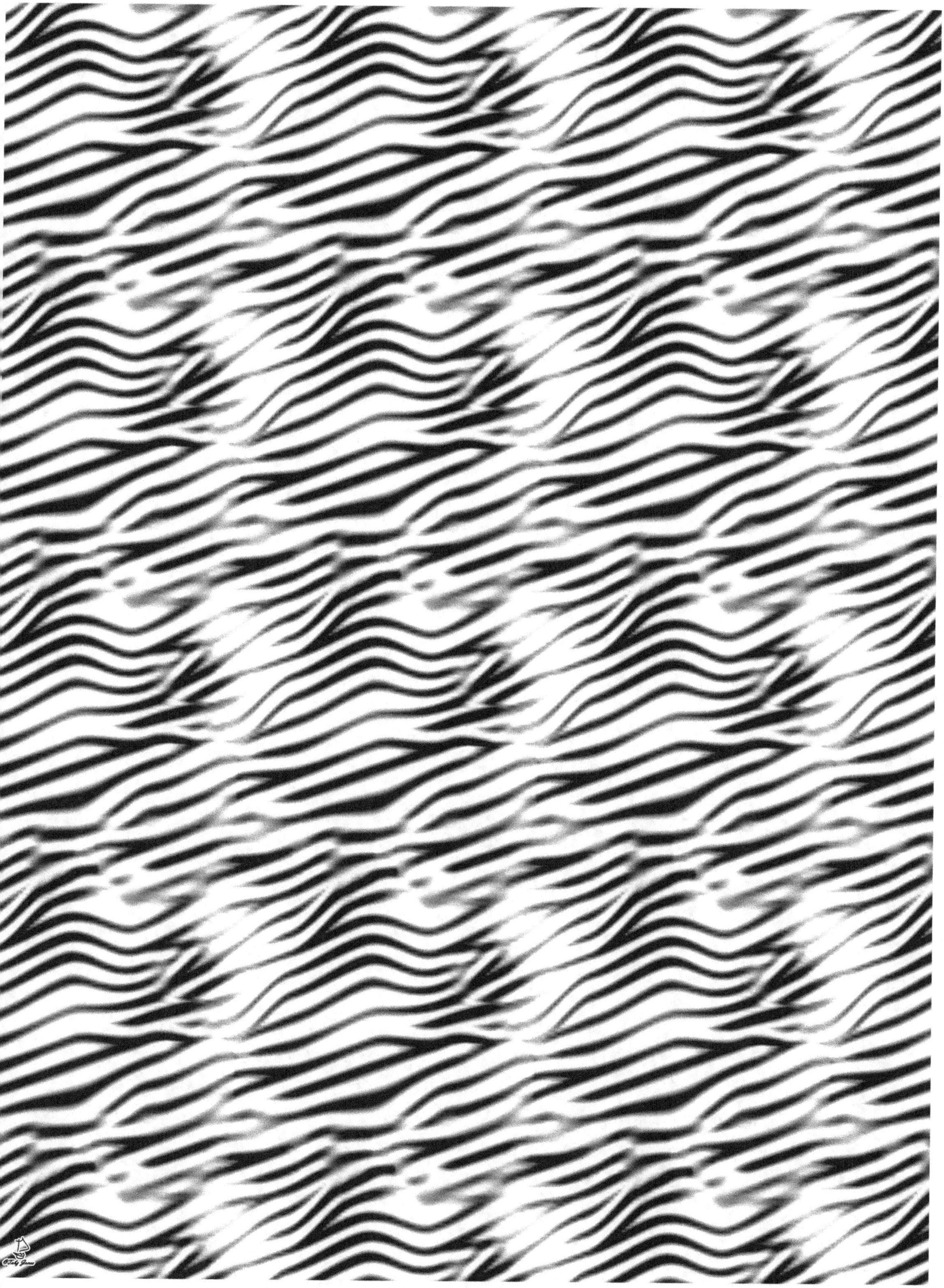
©Toby James

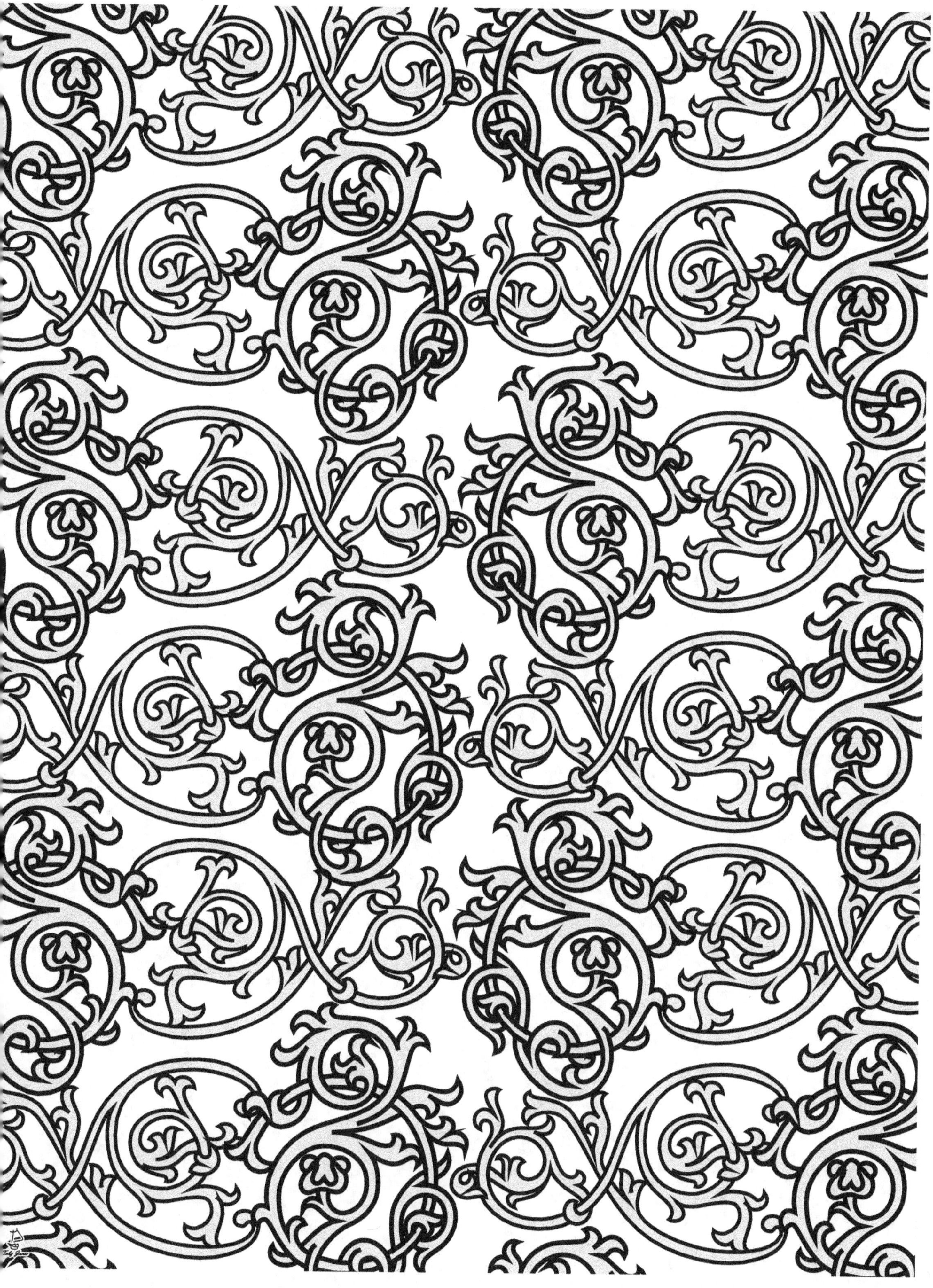

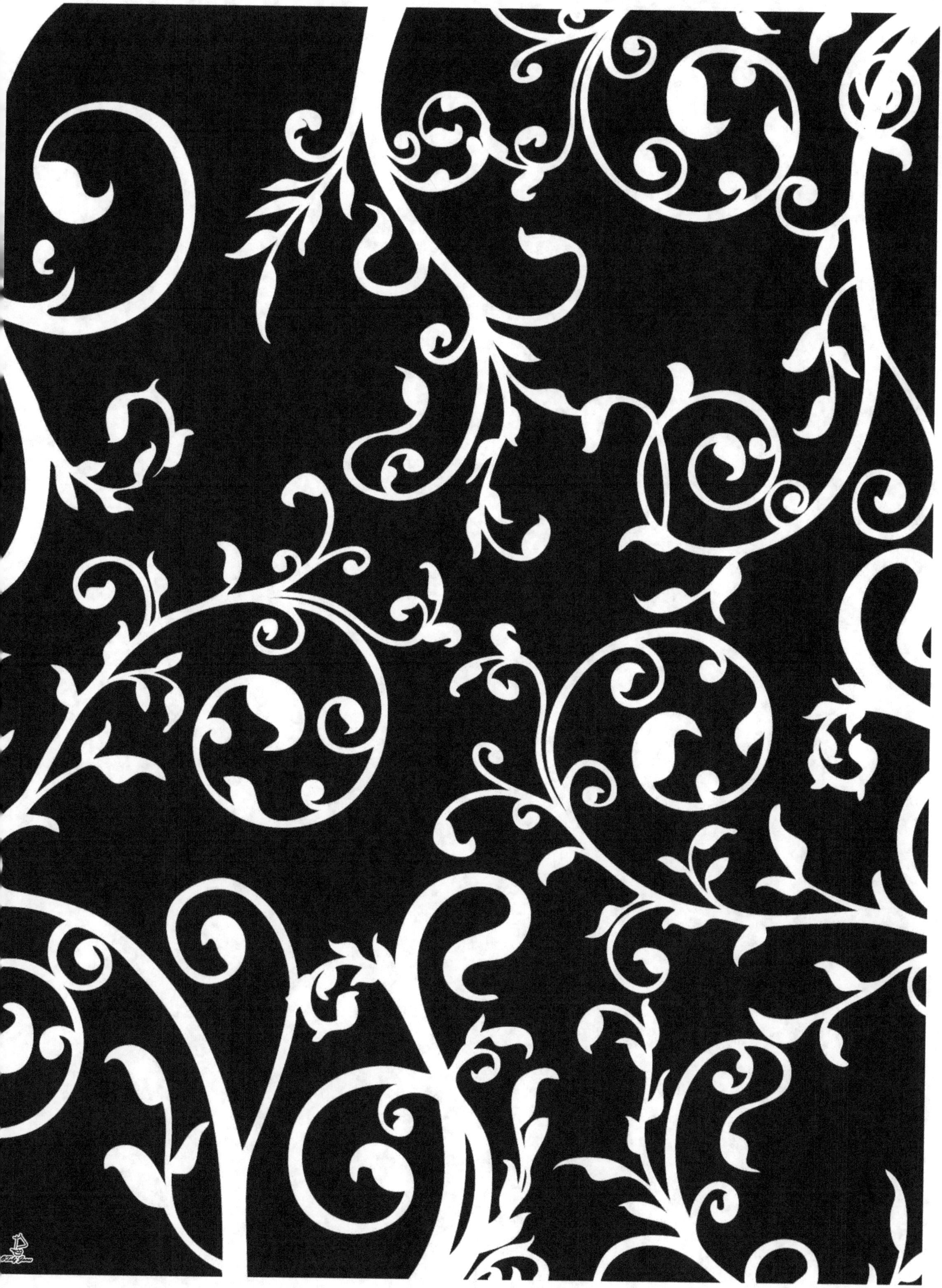

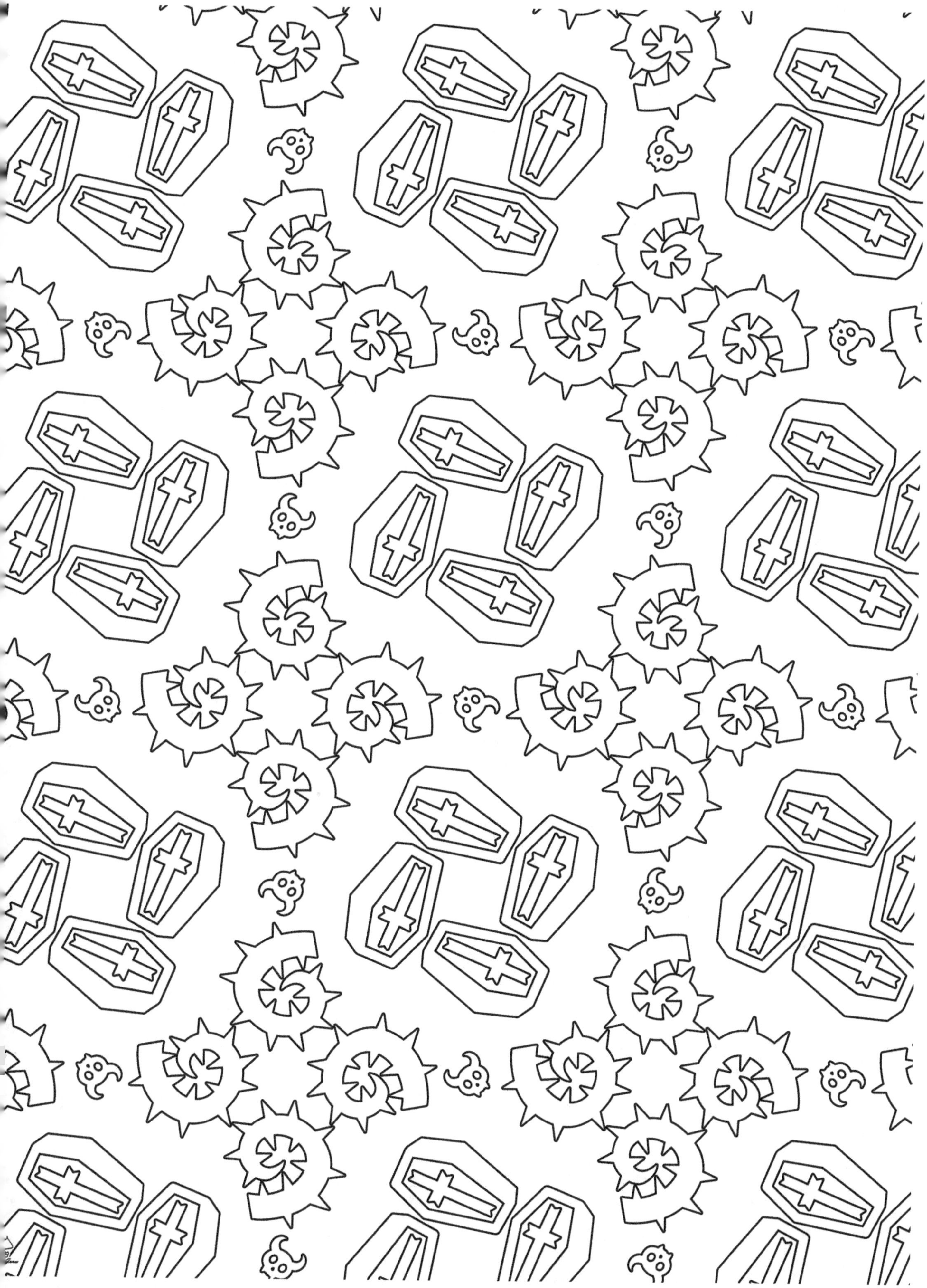

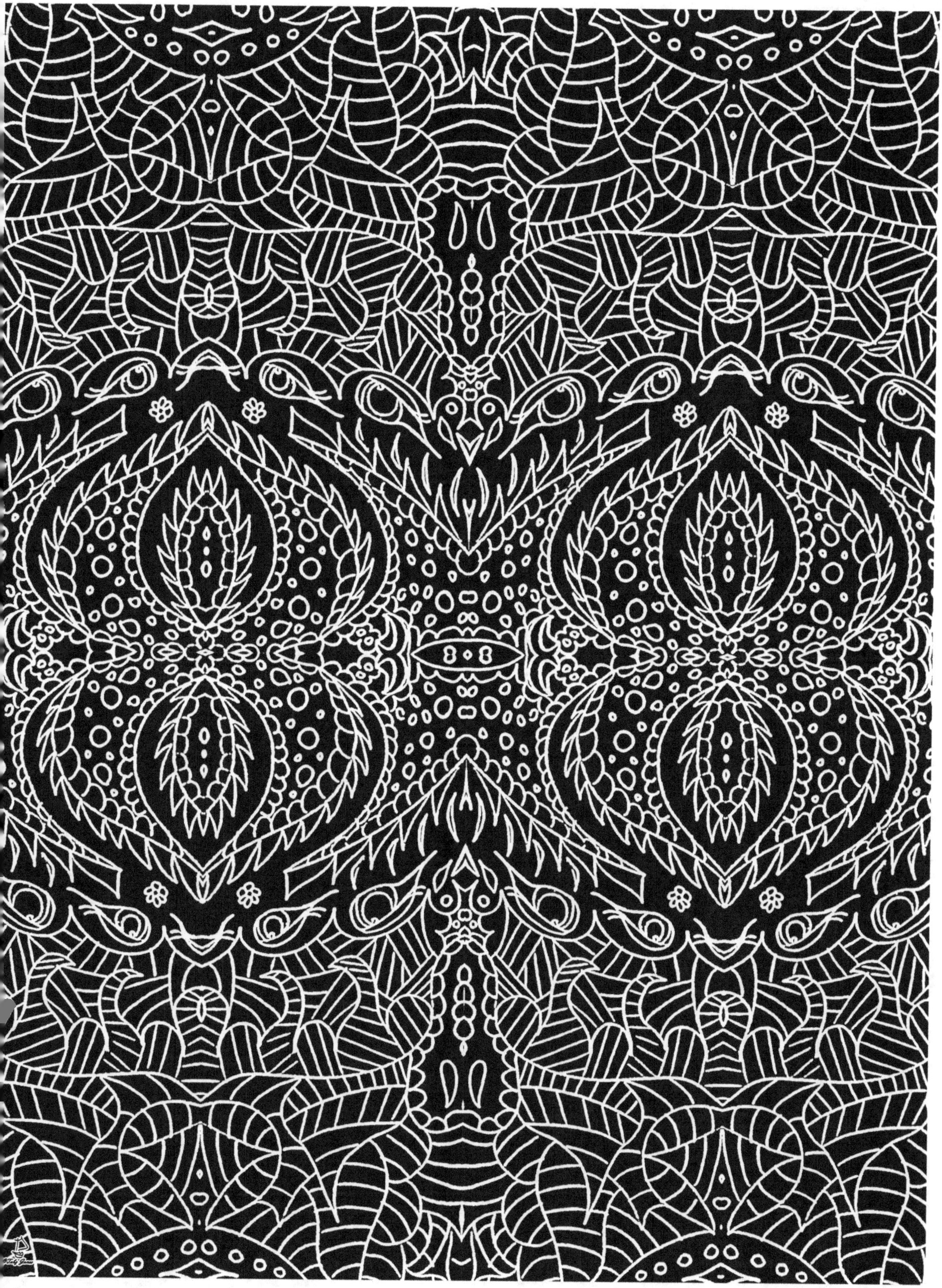

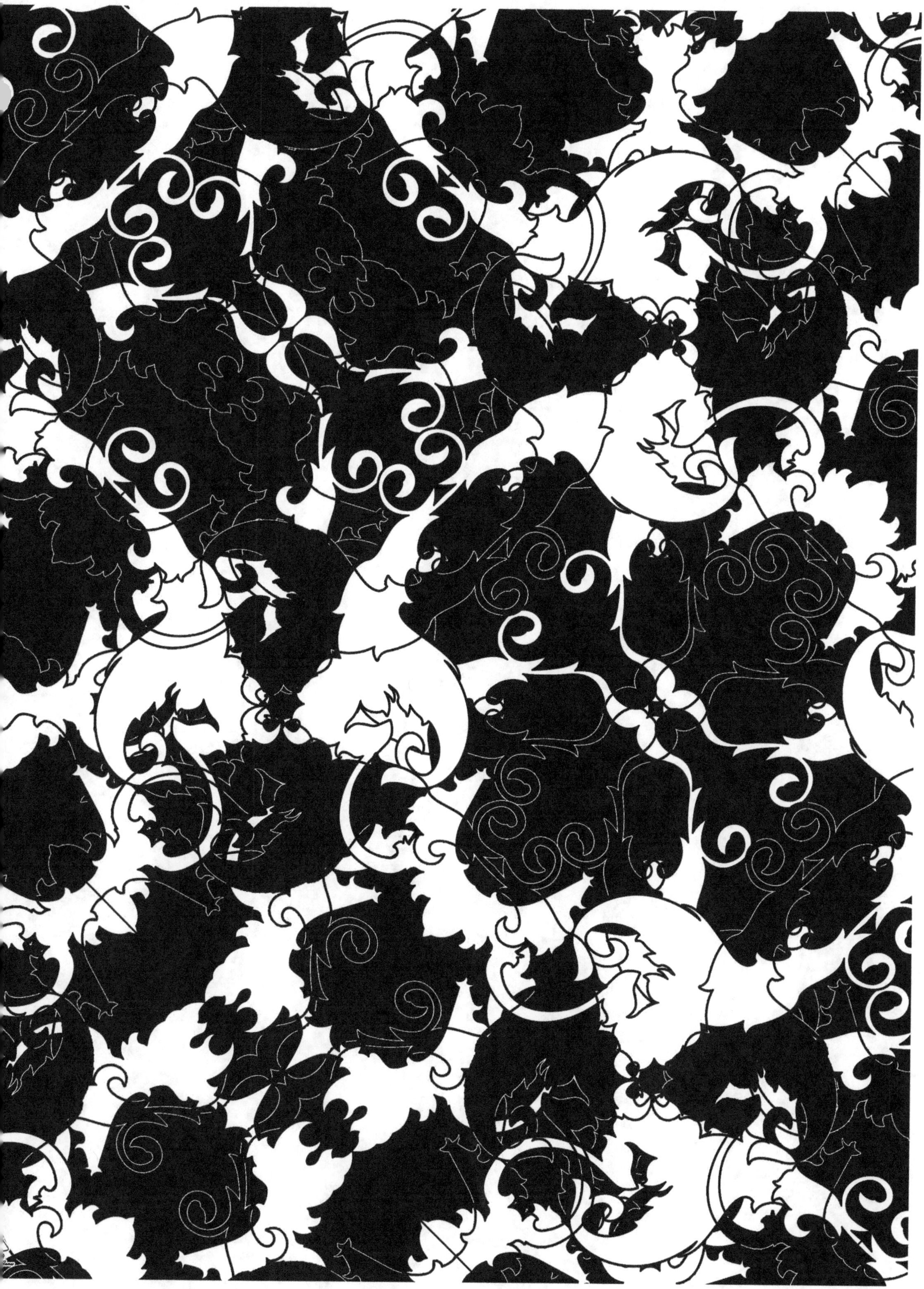

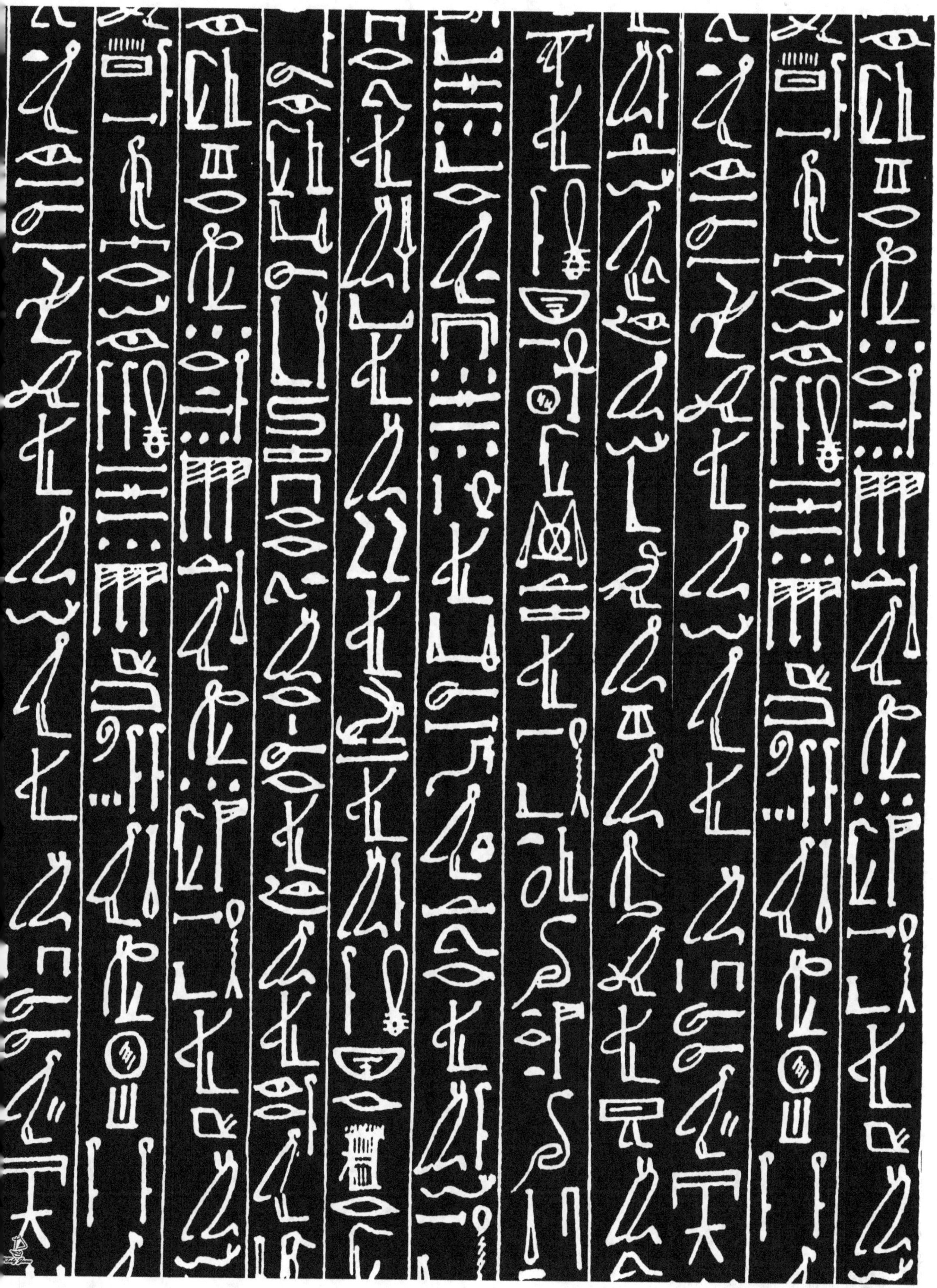

www.ingramcontent.com/pod-product-compliance
Lightning Source LLC
Chambersburg PA
CBHW080607240526
45468CB00030B/2508
* 9 7 8 1 9 7 3 9 9 8 4 2 6 *